D1498404

Easter Basket Stuffers: I Spy Easter Book For Kids Ages 2-5:

A Cute Picture Book with Fun Interactive Guessing Games for Toddlers and Preschoolers (Easter Gifts For Kids)

This Book Belongs to:

_____

_____

Easter is the celebration of the resurrection of Jesus Christ. It is a time of joy and hope, marked by the decoration and the hunting of Easter eggs, which symbolize a new life, and a new beginning.

So who is ready for an Easter adventure with this book?

HOW TO PLAY:
See the pictures and find the item that starts with the letter given.
Look on the next page for the answer.
Color the pictures, and Good luck!

I SPY with my little eye something beginning with...

APPLE

I SPY with my little eye something beginning with...

B

BUNNY

I SPY with my little eye something beginning with...

CHICK

I SPY with my little eye something beginning with...

DUCK

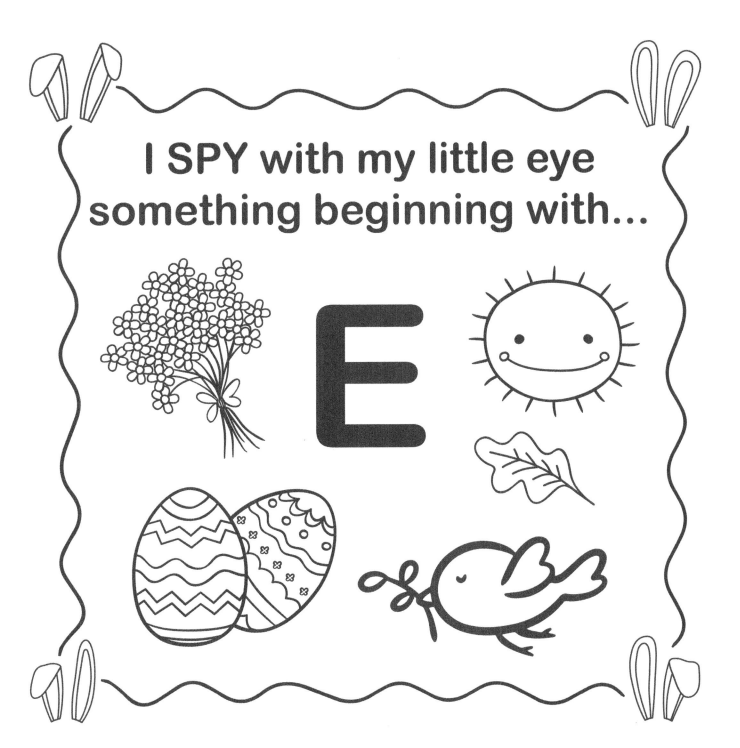

I SPY with my little eye something beginning with...

23

EGGS

I SPY with my little eye something beginning with...

FLOWER

I SPY with my little eye
something beginning with...

G

GIFT

I SPY with my little eye something beginning with...

H

HEN

I SPY with my little eye something beginning with...

ICE CREAM

I SPY with my little eye something beginning with...

JAM

I SPY with my little eye something beginning with...

KETTLE

I SPY with my little eye something beginning with...

LETTER

I SPY with my little eye something beginning with...

MOUSE

I SPY with my little eye something beginning with...

NEST

I SPY with my little eye something beginning with...

OSTARA

I SPY with my little eye something beginning with...

PIE

I SPY with my little eye something beginning with...

QUILL

I SPY with my little eye something beginning with...

R

HAPPY Easter

I SPY with my little eye something beginning with...

S

SHEEP

I SPY with my little eye something beginning with...

T

Happy Easter

TOYS

I SPY with my little eye something beginning with...

U

HAPPY

Easter

UMBRELLA

I SPY with my little eye something beginning with...

VASE

94

I SPY with my little eye something beginning with...

WREATH

I SPY with my little eye something beginning with...

XMAS

I SPY with my little eye something beginning with...

YOGURT

I SPY with my little eye something beginning with...

Z

HAPPY EASTER

ZEBRA

Made in the USA
Monee, IL
20 February 2023